Contents

Every day, all over the world,
people want to know what is going on.

They watch TV.

They listen to the radio.

They read a newspaper.

A lot of the news is all about the present but history is often in the news too.

Sometimes new things are discovered about the past. Sometimes old buildings or objects are in the news.

All the headlines in this book were taken from real newspapers. Many of the news stories were on TV too.

Grisly find is school bonus

● One of the junior school skeletons

A village school project has turned into one of the best local archaeological discoveries on record.

Expert Graham Scobie called it "an extremely important find" this week after lifting a Saxon skeleton found in the grounds of Itchen Abbas Junior School.

And excited school head David Houghton, who launched the project, said: "It is not only important archaeologically, it's a most comprehensive way of learning."

Even more exciting was the discovery alongside of a second skeleton, probably an older man, and a coin buried with him at the time.

"We were sure something was there after a trench dug a couple of years ago showed signs of remains," said Mr Houghton.

"I thought further research would make a good project but I never expected anything like this."

Early hints suggested that the first grave was Christian burial while the second, much deeper and facing the opposite direction, was Pagan.

But now Mr Scobie is sure they were both Pagan and dating back to around 450 AD.

Facts suggest that the first skeleton was a young man of around 21 whose death is still a mystery.

Death for the second man was likely to have been natural causes he said. The skeleton was probably of an older man who was buried with his socks on. For Mr Scobie's team found hobnails from foot-wear.

● Schoolchildren Stuart Swift, Stuart Butler and Daniel Frost help archaeologist Graham Scobie uncover one of the skeleton finds.

Pictures by Mike Englefield

Crafty way to the future

BUILDING a future takes on a new meaning this week when Eastleigh College of Further Education once again becomes regional centre for the Construction Industry's 1986 Induction programme.

First stage of a two-part training scheme, the two week induction course caters for a complete cross section of new trainees ranging from building operatives, trainee craftsmen through to technicians whose role will be to prepare and supervise.

Heavily biased towards safety training and the transition from school life into the new world of work, the programme was first launched at Eastleigh College three years ago.

And as the Construction Industry Training Board's Youth Train-ing Scheme claims it as a major source of success, many other colleges throughout the country are adopting similar schemes.

Bronze

Among the local successes was a bronze medal in carpentry and joinery from City and Guilds of London Institute to local trainee Richard Trott.

EXTRA

3

One of the junior school skeletons.

Grisly find is school bonus

A village school
has

This school found itself in the news.
When a new gas pipe was laid across their field,
the fitters found two ancient skeletons.

The teachers called in some archaeologists. Their job is to look for history clues under the ground.

They dug up some coins, some nails from a pair of boots, a dagger and part of an old belt.

They said the skeletons were of people buried around the year 500 A.D.

Itchen Abbas Junior School, Winchester, 1986

The children kept a record of all the finds on their computer.

Later they read some books to find out more about life long ago.

They talked about what they had found out to a TV crew and had their picture in the paper too.

Shakespeare's Globe unearthed

In London more interesting clues about the past were found under the ground.

There were once two theatres on this site. One was called 'The Rose', the other was called 'The Globe'.

Four hundred years ago William Shakespeare wrote plays to be acted in the theatres.

Globe Theatre, Southwark, 1989

The archaeologists only had a short time to look at the clues and draw a plan.

Here is their drawing.

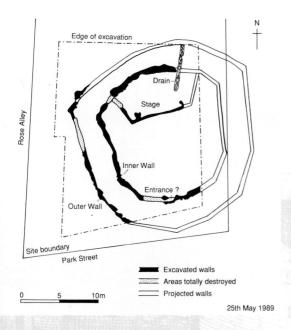

Swan Theatre, London, 1596

Here is a picture of the Swan theatre drawn four hundred years ago.

Afterwards the builders moved in to put up a new office block. Some people wrote to the newspapers.

They said the old theatres should not have been covered up.

What do you think?

Runners give Roman wall the shakes

Roman soldiers built this wall.

For nearly two thousand years, people in Chester have walked round the path on top of the wall.

Today it is in the news because of a round-the-wall race. When six hundred runners all ran round at the same time, some of the bricks in this ancient wall began to move.

Chester people said,

"We don't want our wall to fall down.
The Council must stop the race."

Historic houses fall into ruins

Belle View farmhouse, Lancashire

People moved from this farm twenty years ago.

Old buildings are often in the news.
Some people think they should all
be pulled down.
Others think they should be saved.

A lot of money is needed to repair
these old buildings.

Which ones would you save?

Which ones would you leave
to fall down?

Sinai Park, Staffordshire, 1977

This big house was built four hundred years ago.

Highcliffe castle, Dorset

Part of this castle is six hundred years old.

Daimler, 1930

LOOKING BACK

This old car is up for sale, but it is too expensive for most people to buy. Now it costs £10,500. In 1930, when it was a new car, it cost about £500.

This steam train is usually kept in a museum. Today it is out on the rails again because it is a special anniversary. Fifty years ago it travelled at 126 miles per hour and broke a world speed record. People have come to see it run again.

York station, 1988

Garrett Suffolk Punch steam tractor

This old steam tractor was built in 1919. Today it is going to a steam rally. Can you see the steam? Coal is burnt in the boiler to heat the water which makes the steam. The steam drives the engine.

13

Historic rail station heads for buffers

In 1825 the first train went from Stockton to Darlington.

John Dobbin, 1825

Stockton station was the first railway station, so it is very historic. Now it is in the news again because it is falling down.

Stockton station, 1988

Departure time for disused station as BR offers it at £1 to railway enthusiasts

Leicester station, Humberstone Rd., 1989

Trains stopped here in Leicester for over a century.

In 1968 the station was closed.
Now it is in the news because
it is for sale.

A railway preservation society
wants to buy it and rebuild it
somewhere else.
The old station will be saved.

FOR SALE

OAR-INSPIRING REPLICA

THE long ships are back. This 25-ton Viking warship will set sail as part of the celebrations to commemorate Dublin's Millennium, *writes Simon de Bruxelles.*

Ten unemployed local shipwrights devoted three months to creating the 100ft long replica of a Gokstad-class ocean-going long ship now preserved in a Norwegian museum. Before its maiden voyage this month, secret sea trials are to be held in the coming week at East Wall, at the mouth of the river Liffey.

'We want to know if she is going to keel over before the official launch,' said Ted Courtney, the project's technical adviser.

'The Vikings founded Dublin in the ninth century and the men who built our long ship, the Dyfflin, are descended from those settlers. Many people said it couldn't be done, but everything has gone without a hitch.'

Before she can be launched, the Dyfflin — Norse for the 'black pool', or Dubh Linn, which became Dublin — will have to be manhandled 100 yards to the shore on greased poles.

Replica of Viking warship Dyffl

The two men in this picture are shipwrights. They helped build the big ship. It's a new ship, but an exact copy of one built by the Vikings one thousand years ago.

The Vikings sailed from Norway to Dublin in a ship like this.

The shipwrights want to see if their ship will sail or sink when it goes onto the sea.

Flight Pattern

Scampton, Lincolnshire, 1989

Red Arrow flying teams have put on displays for twenty-five years.

This picture was in the news on the anniversary of the first display.

These pilots were only babies when the first team went into the air. Now they fly their planes in formation just like the pilots did then.

Auctioneer Robin Fenner with Sydney Taylor's camera collection, Tavistock, Devon, 1989

Snapping up a bargain

This collection of old cameras is in the news because they are all for sale.
There are 120 altogether and the oldest was made in 1898.

Lots of people collect toy cars. Some of these are over seventy years old. They were part of a sale of old toys held in London. Look how they have been sorted out into sets.

Christmas broadcasts

The Queen is often in the news.
Every Christmas Day she makes
a special broadcast.
It has become a tradition.
When her grandfather was king,
he made the first Christmas
broadcast in 1932. He spoke on
the radio because no one had television.

Look at the Queen in
1952 when she made
her first broadcast.

Five years later she
went on the television.

This is how she looked
in 1988.

The Queen, TV broadcast, 1988

Children go 'below stairs' to see history in action

Have you ever dressed up like someone who lived in the past?

These children spent a day like children one hundred and fifty years ago.

They made pens called quill pens from feathers.

Then they tried writing with them.

They learnt how to be servants at the big house in the picture.

Saffron Walden schoolchildren at Wimpole Hall, 1988

Victorian school

These children had their photo in the newspaper when they went to an old school.

The school is now in a museum.

After the lesson they went to work in a factory, just like the children who went to this school over a hundred years ago.

Bradford Museum, 1989

William conquers again. . .

These children made their own costumes. They went to a castle for a pretend battle.

Some actors played parts as Saxon and Norman knights.

Their swords and shields looked just like those made one thousand years ago. They were made of cardboard, so no one in the battle would really get hurt.

Stansted Mountfitchet Castle, Essex, 1987